Dan

What makes us human?

And other questions about God,
Jesus and human identity

Thank you for friendship

and  _encouragements_

Mark Meynell

June '16

the good book
COMPANY

What makes us human?
And other questions about God, Jesus and human identity
Part of the *Questions Christians Ask* series
© Mark Meynell/The Good Book Company, 2015.

Published by
The Good Book Company
Tel (UK): 0333 123 0880
Tel (North America): 866 244 2165
International: +44 (0) 208 942 0880
Email (UK): info@thegoodbook.co.uk
Email (North America): info@thegoodbook.com

Websites
UK & Europe: www.thegoodbook.co.uk
North America: www.thegoodbook.com
Australia: www.thegoodbook.com.au
New Zealand: www.thegoodbook.co.nz

Unless otherwise indicated, Scripture quotations are from The Holy Bible, New International Version, NIV Copyright © 1973, 1978, 1984, 2011 by Biblica, Inc. Used by permission. All rights reserved worldwide.

All rights reserved. Except as may be permitted by the Copyright Act, no part of this publication may be reproduced in any form or by any means without prior permission from the publisher.

ISBN: 9781909919051

Printed and bound by CPI Group (UK) Ltd, Croydon, CR0 4YY
Design by André Parker
Graphics: Luke Waldock and André Parker

Contents

To Mum and Dad

Always indebted for laughter, love and life

Introduction

Who am I? At first sight you might be tempted to dismiss this question as something that only angst-ridden teenagers and wild-eyed backpackers ask as they toil to the summit of a Tibetan mountain, in search of a guru with answers.

And certainly many of us go through that experience in early life as we try to work out how like or unlike our parents we want to be, and as we explore what we should believe, test our gifts and abilities, and try to find our place in work, friendships and faith.

But at a more fundamental level, what might seem like a rather abstract philosophical question is actually something of vast and crucial importance to many of the issues that trouble and concern us day by day.

Questions of personal ethics, human rights and sexuality. Questions of economics, war, family and close relationships. Questions about right and wrong, who we are, and how we view other people. The answers we give in all these areas are shaped, deep down, by our answer to this fundamental question: *What is a human being?*

What I understand to be the answer to that question will determine both massive and mundane choices that I make each day.

- *Should I marry him, or should I stay single?*

- *Should I turn off my mother's life-support machine, or should I insist that it is kept on?*

- *Should I feel guilty and ashamed about how I treated her, or should I just shrug it off?*

- *Who should I vote for in the election?*

- *What should I eat for dinner?*

- *Which TV show should I watch?*

As the first chapter shows, you might be surprised to discover that this question—*What is a human being?*—lies at the heart of a huge and largely invisible argument that is raging in our culture: in politics, in the media and in private conversations. And it is a question that followers of Jesus need to be clear about how to answer if we are to understand the times, engage meaningfully in discussion with others and make choices that honour God.

The good news is that the Bible has a lot to say about who we are, and what makes us human. It tells us we are creatures, not coincidence. It tells us that we are precious, not pointless. It shows where we came from and where we are going to. It tells us we are dust, but that we are dust with a destiny.

And ultimately, it reveals to us a man who is the measure of what it means to be truly human. A man whose perfect humanity meant he was able to be a substitute who put right all that is wrong with a world of men and women at odds with God and themselves.

Tim Thornborough
Series Editor, June 2015

Chapter 1

Who on earth are we?

This is a short book about a big subject. A *very* big subject in fact—US!

But don't think it's big because we're egomaniacs—although some of us clearly are! It's a big subject because we're *complicated*. There's so much to us, much more than meets the eye.

That's why couples who have been married for decades still find surprising things to learn about each other. That's why we sometimes will surprise ourselves when we say or do something that doesn't fit in with who we think we are.

It turns out that people are not so much problems to be solved, but mysteries to be explored and enjoyed.

Isn't that one of the reasons why people are so fascinating? Sometimes it's fun to sit at a cafe table and watch the world go by, quietly taking in everyone's interactions and quirks while you sip your latte. You pick up intriguing slices of conversation that hint at a whole world you know nothing about.

It's fun precisely because *we're all so different*—racially, culturally, socially, educationally, generationally, intellectually, psychologically, physically. It doesn't matter what aspect I choose, it's guaranteed that my "normal" will be someone else's "totally bizarre" somewhere on earth.

Yet here's the astonishing fact. For all the countless ways in which we set ourselves apart from others, we always have far more in common than we realise.

It's perhaps more vital than ever to tackle this question now, since the modern world offers so many options. They don't just contradict each other; they also conflict with what Christians have historically believed from the Bible.

This matters. How we understand ourselves profoundly shapes how we treat one another: when others' skin is darker or lighter, their gender or religion or marital status is different, or they are weaker or less educated or sicker or poorer, or they have yet to be born or have limited brain function.

So, before we consider the Bible's take, we'll think briefly about five different approaches that keep cropping up today. I'm sure you'll recognise them.

As we think about these alternative approaches, one danger we must constantly be alert to is what is called "reductionism". We've already seen that human beings are complicated. Reductionism always tries to oversimplify reality by reducing it to a single principle, or a few sound bites. The giveaway words are when someone says that a certain aspect of human behaviour is "just *this*" or is "nothing but *that*". An eminent scientist and Christian, Donald Mackay, coined the phrase "nothing buttery" for reductionism. The problem is that it's a tendency that even Christians are prone to, as we'll see.

1. MINDS: *Humans as thinkers*

"I think, therefore I am."

The French philosopher René Descartes was one of the greatest minds of all time. He wanted to know how we could be sure about what is true. So he set himself the task of finding a set of principles about which there could be absolutely no doubts. But to do this, he doubted all kinds of things that people unthinkingly assume are true—like whether we exist or not.

His momentous conclusion was that the only things truly beyond doubt were the thoughts flowing through his mind. We can't always trust what others around us tell us. And we can't always trust our own views about the world around us. Our fellow humans and our own physical senses often play tricks on us. All that's left are the conclusions we come to in our own minds. We have our reason.

Because it's impossible to separate thoughts from the person thinking them, Descartes arrived at his famous statement. I can know I exist because I know I am thinking, or more famously: **"I think, therefore I am"**. So even the fact that I might doubt the truth of a statement proves my own existence.

So then, what can we know for certain? Who on earth are we? Descartes's answer is that we are *thinkers*. We are people who are able to process ideas, and to act in the world on the basis of what we've considered.

We are thinking beings: animals are not. Therefore we are justified in eating them and treating them differently. But it's quite a limited definition, when you stop to think about it. Here are some questions it side steps.

■ *What about other people? How can I be sure they exist? They could simply be figments of my own active imagination—as if the simulated reality experienced by humans in the movie* The Matrix *was actually operating in my mind! What's to stop my reality becoming totally cocooned from everything around me?*

■ *What about my body? Is it just incidental to who I am? Perhaps it's even a restrictive inconvenience, especially when it stops me thinking rationally—as when I've had too many beers or am under too much stress.*

■ *And what about my reason? What actually makes me so sure I can get stuff right, even without my manipulative passions and flawed perceptions? Human reason is hardly as stable or reliable as some might hope. Hasn't history proved that some of the most rational people can still be the most flawed?*

So perhaps it might help to look outside ourselves for more rounded views of who and what we are...

2. APES: *Humans as animals*

"Human beings are nothing but upright animals with a taste for clothes and complicated food."

Jane Goodall is renowned for her remarkable and sometimes controversial work with East African chimpanzees. With great courage and painstaking research, she has popularized the idea that we share many characteristics with apes. So in chimps, Goodall has observed personalities, emotions and perhaps even some rational thought. They certainly show remarkable social behaviour, with hugs and tickling, familial affection and memory.

Genetic research has shown that chimps share between 95 and 99% of human DNA. This is why some scientists can make this kind of claim:

Darwin wasn't just provocative in saying that we descend from the apes—he didn't go far enough. We are apes in every way, from our long arms and tailless bodies to our habits and temperament.
National Geographic, August 2005

The most powerful wildlife film I've ever seen follows the visit of conservationist Damian Aspinall to the West African jungles of Gabon. He wanted to track down Kwibi, a gorilla that had grown up with Aspinall at a conservation trust before his introduction into the wild, aged five. Eventually, they found him. No one knew how Kwibi, now a fully-grown ten-year old, would respond. With threats or even violence?

But Kwibi recognised Aspinall instantly. He embraced him and wouldn't let him go! He then "introduced" his family, who gathered to watch. When the camera team were eventually able to extricate themselves in a boat, Kwibi followed them along the riverbank and slept overnight with his family on the opposite bank. It was a remarkable demonstration of just how similar we are.

So perhaps we really are just animals, albeit rather more developed, or more evolved? It does seem possible to have a genuine relationship of sorts with them, perhaps even at a deep level. Dog and cat owners would all testify to that (and we share 90% of DNA with cats and 80% with dogs).

While all this is undeniable, does it actually get us anywhere in establishing who *we* are? After all, we also share 50% of our DNA with bananas, but few would suggest this helps! We might all be "half-banana" at the microscopic level, but we have precious little else in common—apart from becoming a trip hazard if we are left lying around.

Yet even if human biology does share this much with the animal world, does *nothing* distinguish us from the animal kingdom? There are three substantial things that we can point to:

- ▪ *Levels of communication: Surely there's a **qualitative** difference between our respective abilities to communicate. Consider the complexities of human language: it can be so nuanced, flexible and multi-layered. Just read a Shakespeare sonnet to see that. That's of an order far removed from the glories of the* *dawn chorus or a mammal's ability to warn its group of a predator.*

■ ***Animal instinct:*** *Why is it wise to visit an African game park with a professionally trained warden? It's because wild animals are* dangerous. *How can lions or hippos be anything else? They can't be expected to be "responsible" or even "reasonable", especially when they spot a potential threat or the next meal. It is one of the facts of (wild)life. As Tennyson rightly pointed out, nature really is "red in tooth and claw".*

■ ***Human responsibility:*** *We're so much greater than the sum of our ingrained or learned instincts. We can't simply excuse any behaviour as a symptom of our genetic make-up or subconscious instincts. Our nature or our nurture may help to explain, of course. But the entire criminal justice system would be rendered irrelevant if these provided a total excuse. Nobody could be held responsible for anything. How would the victims of rape or violent assault feel then?*

These kinds of questions show the problem at the heart of the simple statement "we are nothing but animals". Many people would say this, but it is not how they feel or behave. When great athletes achieve great feats, isn't it remarkable how few brush off compliments and accolades by saying: "It was just my genes, you know"?

Inherited physical attributes and predispositions are undoubtedly important. For example, I don't have anything like Usain Bolt's thighs, Lionel Messi's ball skills or Michael Phelps' lung capacity. But just as important as these inherited traits are the will-power, ambition, and stamina that need to be deployed to make a great athlete. Not to mention the wealth and opportunities to train with the best.

We want to have our cake and eat it.

We must beware of "nothing-buttery". We certainly do have lots in common with animals so that we must never be seen as less than them. But surely we're so much more, aren't we?

3. COMPUTERS: *Humans as biological machines*

> *"I regard the brain as a computer which will stop working when its components fail. There is no heaven or afterlife for broken down computers; that is a fairy story for people afraid of the dark."*
> STEPHEN HAWKING

This is almost the polar opposite of humans as animals. Instead of fellow mammals, we find analogies in the man-made. Think about it. Aren't there more than a few similarities between human brains and computers?

- *Brains and computers both use electrical signals to send messages for which they need energy (the former using chemical reactions rather than electricity).*

- *Both have expandable memory (with brains adding stronger synaptic connections and computers adding more chips).*

- *Both can multitask (though some brains are perhaps better than others at this!).*

■ *Both can learn from trial and error.*

■ *Both can get damaged, with unpredictable conse-quences.*

The list goes on. This is subtly different from Descartes's argument about thinking. It's about all the things the brain does, whether we're conscious of them or not.

Computers are developing all the time with breath-taking speed—unlike the human brain. Back in 1965, Intel's Gordon E. Moore predicted that the number of transistors within a computer chip would double every two years. Moore's Law (as it was soon dubbed) proved remarkably accurate.

So in August 2014, IBM unveiled a brand new prod-uct with a deliberately neurological-sounding name: a neurosynaptic chip they called TrueNorth. It has almost quadruple the number of transistors of previous chips (with 5.4 billion) and has a million neurons. If that seems meaningless, it squeezes the power of a super-computer into the space of a postage stamp. It's incredible.

TrueNorth is not a human brain—we each have 100 billion neurons and up to 150 trillion synapses. IBM still has a long way to go! But with the development of True-North, the possibility of human-like artificial intelligence looms ever closer. All kinds of claims have been made for various machines in recent years—but senior researchers have dismissed these as nonsense, while acknowledging that "it will happen eventually". The ideas of science fic-tion (as in films like *2001: A Space Odyssey*; *I, Robot*; and *Ex Machina*) seem to be becoming "science fact".

So it is easy to see why people can think that we are simply biological computers wired into physical bodies. And if that is all we are, why not invest in some strategic upgrades? That's the appeal of a new movement called *transhumanism* (or H+ as it is sometimes known). As technology develops, we will surely be able to transcend our intellectual, psychological and physical limitations. Advocates claim that this is simply the next triumphant stage in human evolution.

Of course, it's already been happening for years, from hip replacements to pacemakers and in-vitro fertilisation. So aren't other "upgrades", such as stem-cell-derived organs, mechanical hands controlled by brain impulses and perhaps even memory-chip implants, only different in degree? Many of these medical advances are clearly beneficial and even life-transforming. How can a sighted person possibly object to someone who has never seen receiving optical implants?

But are there any limits to what we can improve? And more to the point, might the limitations we all share not be so detrimental after all?

Perhaps it might all be a bit like those who get addicted to cosmetic surgery. At the start, the odd nip or tuck makes clear improvements. For those who have suffered terrible burns or injuries, it can even be a life-saver. But some can't seem to stop once they have started. Rather than grow old gracefully, allowing their faces to look lived in and experienced, they become increasingly plastic and even grotesque. In the worst cases, they come to look more like waxwork dummies than real people.

Might not our very earthy bodily limitations actually

be integral to what it means to be human somehow? And could there be a point beyond which someone ceases to be fully human? These are knotty problems which are beyond the scope of this book.

But what if the initial premise of the analogy with the computer is actually flawed and unhelpful? For isn't there so much more to human life than the magnificent complexity of the brain?

There are aspects to our humanity that are not precisely logical, binary or rational—and despite our imperfections, that's actually no bad thing. In *Star Trek*, when Spock says to Kirk: "That's illogical, captain," it does not always make Kirk wrong as far as the plotline is concerned. Aspects of our humanity, like creativity or compassion, can never be reduced to lines of code. What's more, our physicality is surely as integral to our humanness as our consciousness, as we will now discover...

4. TOOLS: *Humans as economic resources*

"When I was a kid I always wondered what drove ants to line up and work all day for the queen. Now I work a boring job all day for low pay so that execs can get millions. I'm just an ant in traffic."
ANONYMOUS COMMENT ON A BLOG POST

Meet someone new and what do you ask? First, for their name. Then about their work. At one level, the latter is a perfectly innocent question. Yet how often do we instinctively pigeonhole people on the basis of their answer?

A brain surgeon seems far more significant than

someone on a supermarket checkout. But that only proves how much we've been swayed by our culture. We've measured human worth by the same yardstick as the market: greater abilities equal greater value. After all, the market always pays the going rates for different skills. That's how capitalism works.

In the West, we've been brought up on the story of capitalism's victory over communism in the twentieth century. It's now the only viable economic system, apparently. And it works: people become incredibly rich as a result. Or perhaps, to be more accurate, some people do. At the time of writing, it was calculated that for the first time in history, 1% of the world's population was on course to own more than the other 99%. That may not seem particularly significant, until you contrast it with the 2.2 billion people who live on less than US$2 a day (a World Bank benchmark for deep deprivation).

The question, then, is: *are those 2 billion lives worth less?* In economic terms, they certainly are. But in human terms? Do they not share some innate human traits with those of us who live on far more than $2 a day? I hope we would all readily agree that they do.

And yet the way the world functions today proves that in practice they are not as valuable as Western lives. Consider the global outcry after the attacks on the Paris offices of the satirical magazine *Charlie Hebdo*, in which fifteen people died. But in the same week, Boko Haram massacred 2000 Nigerians. Where was the global outrage? When did presidents gather to march in solidarity? There is something profoundly unsettling about that. And it happens all the time.

A person's value is reduced to his or her net contribution to the finances of a company or a country. That's why corporations faced with difficult decisions tend only to consider profit margins. It makes decisions about outsourcing or relocation far clearer. Directors routinely plan on the basis of efficiency, rather than moral or social responsibility. Outsourcing production to Bangalore may create huge savings—but at the same time shatter a whole town's survival.

The kind of language that reduces humans to their economic utility infiltrates so much more of modern life. Value for money is, of course, an important concern, but it seems to have become the *only* measurement for evaluating education, healthcare, the arts and heritage, the great outdoors, the environment and even relationships.

But the question is actually more sinister than it might first appear. What will happen to those who are seemingly unable to contribute much to society? What about the brain-damaged or physically disabled, those not born yet or too old to live alone safely? Don't they have a legitimate place in society? Or do they forfeit that right because of their impairments, age or lack of potential as consumers or contributors? Few people put arguments for deportation, abortion or euthanasia in such stark terms—but if people are *just* resources, what's to stop a society assuming the right to do away with those who cannot be net contributors?

Put in those terms, reducing a person's value to their abilities is chilling.

We've seen that all these approaches to the question of how we define ourselves seem, at first, to have some attractions. But the more we probe them with questions, the more inadequate they seem. So perhaps in reaction to such "nothing buttery", the only alternative is to give up on facile generalisations altogether.

5. SHRUGS: *Humans as... who knows?!*

> *"No one can comprehend what goes on under the sun. Despite all their efforts to search it out, no one can discover its meaning. Even if the wise claim they know, they cannot really comprehend it."*
> *Ecclesiastes 8 v 17*

Ask a random selection of people who we are, and a number will just shrug their shoulders and say: "Don't know" or: "Who cares?" They might continue, just let people find their own path in life. Find whatever is beautiful or unique or worthy in yourself, and help others to do the same.

After all, isn't life all a matter of deciding what we want to be and then becoming it? As one university strapline advertised: *"University isn't about finding yourself; it's about creating yourself."*

For surely, the argument goes, all the categories that divide us—especially those of gender, sexuality and family—are merely human constructs anyway. Anyone who tells you otherwise is merely trying to impose their oppressive constraints on those who are different from them.

And yet… and yet…

Surely there has to be more to it than this? Surely, what's required is to accept the nuances of human complexity and try to hold it all together somehow?

For all the wonders and ingenuity of the animal kingdom, and the complexities and similarities with computer chips, it seems to require the unique ingenious creativity of human beings to compose Bach's *Well-Tempered Clavier* or The Beatles' *Sergeant Pepper*; to paint Michelangelo's Sistine Chapel frescos or Banksy's street art; to perform *Hamlet* or *Les Misérables*. Neither fleet-footed mammals nor laptop motherboards have anything on us! We are absolutely magnificent! There must be more to us than our consciousness, physicality, biology or neurology. We can't be reduced to any one of these things.

- *We have consciousness… but also passions, instincts, and bodies.*

- *We are mammals… but we also have complex creativity, language and responsibility.*

- *We have incredible brain-power… but also physicality and the capacity for great compassion.*

- *We have great capacities… but also individual, intrinsic value that far exceeds our ability to contribute to society.*

And holding all these competing and contradictory thoughts together is precisely what the Bible helps us to do.

Chapter 2

MADE: *How does God see us?*

Adifferent perspective. That's what I usually need when I get so bogged down in a job that I can't see how to finish it. It might come from simply putting the kettle on and staring out the window for a bit. Or it might come from leaving it to do something completely different for a while.

In fact, isn't that true of so much in life? When things puzzle us and we can't work them out, our first strategy might be to leave it and wait. Time makes such a difference to the way we see things.

Travel also helps. After the privilege of a few years in East Africa, I found I'd grown to love my own country more (it's home), but I had simultaneously become far less patient of nationalism—that kind of patriotism on steroids. This was because I'd found so much to appreciate and love in other countries.

But perhaps our greatest perspective shift comes from realising that there really is a God. It's as if you have lived your whole life indoors without ever going outside. And then suddenly, there's a huge, crashing boom as a gigantic crane hoists the entire roof away. In an instant, everything has changed. For the first time, you can see, hear or feel the sky, the breeze, the sun, the birds—the world that has been carrying on all this time. We can never see ourselves in the same way again.

The alternative views of humanity we've just considered are all defective for one simple reason. They all begin (and end) with *us*. They're just groping in the dark. But lifting the roof off shows us how absurdly narrow-minded that is.

So it is no accident that John Calvin opens his monumental life's work, *The Institutes*, with these words:

> *Nearly all the wisdom we possess, that is to say, true and sound wisdom, consists of two parts: the knowledge of God and of ourselves. (Inst. I 1:1)*

The book you are now reading is not a study of God—rather, it spotlights how we should understand ourselves in the light of God. To grasp how God sees us, we need to read what God has revealed to his world through the writers of the Bible.

1. Made in God's Image: *how we function*

In Genesis chapters 1 and 2, we are given a ringside glimpse of God's spectacular creation of the cosmos, culminating in the first man and woman in Eden. This is not the place to get bogged down in the complexities of contemporary debates about this account—and anyway, Genesis is primarily a work of theology, not scientific analysis, although we can be sure it will be entirely consistent with the accurate findings of science. Rather, we simply need to ask what theological truths these foundational chapters reveal about human nature. Can we make sense of God's purpose for humanity from this creation blueprint?

After an inventory of "good" things that God has created, he makes a monumental announcement:

> Then God said, "Let us make mankind in our image, in our likeness, so that they may rule over the fish in the sea and the birds in the sky, over the livestock and all the wild animals, and over all the creatures that move along the ground."
> So God created mankind in his own image,
>   in the image of God he created them;
>   male and female he created them.
> God blessed them and said to them, "Be fruitful and increase in number; fill the earth and subdue it. Rule over the fish in the sea and the birds in the sky and over every living creature that moves on the ground." *Genesis 1 v 26-28*

Humanity therefore seems to be a kind of hybrid creature. This explains the continuity with the rest of creation:

■ *We're a created species, placed within the environment of an earthbound garden.*

■ *We're made up of two sexes, male and female.*

■ *We come at the culmination of the creation process.*

All of which undoubtedly explains why we share so many characteristics with other creatures, especially mammals, from our DNA onwards. God clearly found the template of a face with two eyes and ears, one nose and mouth, so effective that he used it many times over.

So we are never less than physical beings, with flesh and blood. We are fragile and earthbound.

And yet, there are some things that set us apart.

The Bible's answer is specific: we are created "in his own image". That suggests that we somehow reflect God in profound and essential ways. This is why we should never be reduced to mere animals driven by instincts and hormones.

Barrels of ink have been spilled over what this word "image" actually means, but let's be clear on this—it's not some tacked-on extra, as if we're slightly upgraded mammals. It is about who we fundamentally are, not about a few upgraded attributes we might possess.

A few significant features flow from this.

We are created for responsibilities

Humanity is made to rule over creation.

> ... so that they may rule over ... all the creatures
> that move along the ground.   *Genesis 1 v 26*

This is obviously not to be *exploitative* domination as some have suggested—after all, to abuse the environment in which we are to thrive is counter-productive. We read in Genesis 2 v 15 that the man was placed in the garden to "work it and take care of it". We are creation's stewards and custodians, not oppressors or parasites. This responsibility is to be passed on to future generations, which explains humanity's mandate to procreate (1 v 28).

We are created for relationships

> So the LORD God caused the man to fall into a deep sleep; and while he was sleeping, he took one of the man's ribs and then closed up the place with flesh. Then the LORD God made a woman from the rib he had taken out of the man, and he brought her to the man.
>
> The man said,
> "This is now bone of my bones
>   and flesh of my flesh;
> she shall be called 'woman',
>   for she was taken out of man."
>
> *Genesis 2 v 21-33*

Following a fruitless search for a "suitable helper" among the other animals, the man is given a partner equally made in God's image. She is equal, but she is *different*: she is female and not male.

When he wakes to discover another person, on exactly the same wavelength as him, he's overjoyed, and bursts out in a song of praise and delight. He has found an end to his loneliness in a horizontal relationship with the woman. But this is complemented by two vertical relationships: *up*, to God the loving Creator, who has authority over us; and *down*, to the rest of creation, over which we are given responsibilities. We could summarise these relationships as:

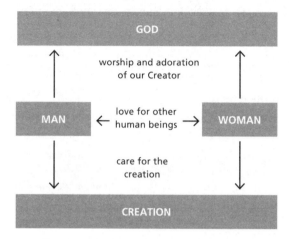

To leave the concept of the image of God there, however, is to commit the same blunder of "nothing buttery" seen in chapter 1. It must mean *at least* these things (as is clear from Genesis chapters 1 and 2) but it cannot mean *only* these things—for many aspects of human nature reflect, however palely, something of God's nature:

- **We have capacities for abstract reasoning and for language** (*although God does accommodate himself to communicate on our level—Isaiah 55 v 8*).

- **We have the capacity for creativity**—*although strictly speaking, we are only rearranging what already exists, in contrast to God's creation out of nothing. But notice how Moses describes God's commission of the craftsman Bezalel in Exodus 35 v 30-33.*

■ *We have the capacity for self-giving (as opposed to instinct-driven) love and compassion. How else could Paul, for example, call on us to love as we have been loved (Ephesians 5 v 1-2)?*

So human beings are a hybrid, unique in all creation. This thought is picked up in Psalm 8 v 5, with the idea of us being "crowned" but also made "a little lower than the angels". We are made from dust, but we are simultaneously embodied souls, made by God in his image, and loved by God as his creation.

2. Made in God's Image: *how we flourish*

Perhaps this seems rather remote. Does it have any bearing on commuting to work, or washing up, or on family dilemmas or old age? Of course it does—but let's listen to King David as he applies these universal truths to his daily experience in Psalm 139. Here are just a few highlights:

> You have searched me, LORD, and you know me.
> *(Psalm 139 v 1)*

David is living life with the roof off. He knows that God sees all his daily activities (v 2-3), reads all his thoughts and hears all his words (v 2, 4). But far from being intimidated by this fact, he is overjoyed, for there's nowhere he can go that is outside God's providential care and love (v 7-9). That includes the times when he is in the pit of despair (v 11-12). But he admits that this God-consciousness in life is hard to get your head around.

> Such knowledge is too wonderful for me, too lofty for me to attain. *(v 6)*

Yet here is the astonishing reality: *God is with him.* But why?! Why would the Creator of the cosmos and Sovereign of history even bother? David's explanation is simple:

> For you created my inmost being; you knit me together in my mother's womb. I praise you because I am fearfully and wonderfully made; your works are wonderful, I know that full well. *(v 13-14)*

We belong to God *because he made us.* And that means we depend on him as much as we belong to him (regardless of whether we recognise those truths). There is not one moment of our lives that escapes his notice. There is not one moment of our existence that he is not there and involved with.

But precisely because we're created, we know we're not biological accidents, lacking purpose or value or meaning. God knows each and every one of us in our humanness and individuality—right down to the number of hairs on our heads (Luke 12 v 7). It really is overwhelming—as David says, it's almost too wonderful to know! Yet God really has made us! And having made us, he has not left us, but remains close and intimately involved in the daily lives of his creatures.

Four key realities flow naturally from this.

God made us for worship:
SO atheism is "folly"

Human beings are worshippers by nature. The question has never been *if*, but *what* will we worship? That's no accident. It's how we're wired: to live in relationship with God. This is the beautiful picture of the man and woman's intimacy with the Lord in the garden. That relationship is as fundamental to human flourishing as oxygen is to our physical health.

And this plain fact explains the Bible's verdict on those who seek to live without God: *sheer folly!*

> The fear of the LORD is the beginning of knowledge, but fools despise wisdom and instruction.
>
> *Proverbs 1 v 7*

> The fool says in his heart, "There is no God."
>
> *Psalm 14 v 1*

Take note: folly is not lacking common sense; nor is it a matter of intelligence; still less is it a matter of appearing religious. Folly is refusing to worship God. The irony is that we can do that both by never darkening the doors of a religious building (the atheist version of folly) and through all kinds of spiritual activity (the religious version). What ultimately matters is who we depend on for our life and flourishing—ourselves or our Maker?

We might tick the Christian boxes on the census form, but be living as a functional atheist. To that, the Bible simply says: "*Fool!*" Jesus makes precisely this point with his parable of the rich fool (Luke 12 v 13-21).

God made us for dependence:
SO we need to trust him

Like an artist who gets to decide what happens to a masterpiece, like parents with their precious child, God has authority over us. We owe him everything—our gifts, our minds, our wealth, our love.

One of the grand deceptions of Western thinking has been that true freedom can only be found through personal independence—too often people *have* been oppressed or exploited by those in power over them. To be freed from that is a matter of justice.

But it's an enormous leap from human power abuses to assuming we're better off without *any* authority—let alone God's authority. Surely it depends on the character and motivations of the one in power? God is entirely dependable, good and generous, especially towards the most vulnerable.

> For the LORD your God is God of gods and Lord of lords, the great God, mighty and awesome, who shows no partiality and accepts no bribes. He defends the cause of the fatherless and the widow, and loves the foreigner residing among you, giving them food and clothing. *Deuteronomy 10 v 17-18*

What's not to like about trusting a God like that?

If you were fortunate enough to grow up with parents who looked after you, protected you and worked to provide for you, you will understand. They wanted you to flourish and grow. And they are weak, fallible and imperfect. And even if you didn't have parents like that, you instinctively know that this is the kind of parent you needed—and want to be yourself.

Jesus tells us that we have a heavenly Father who is so much greater than even the best human parent. He ex-

ercises his authority in a way that fosters human flourishing, protection and growth. Jesus said:

> If you, then, though you are evil, know how to
> give good gifts to your children, how much more
> will your Father in heaven give good gifts to those
> who ask him!   *Matthew 7 v 11*

God put eternity is in our hearts:
SO this life can never fully satisfy

Because we are hybrid creatures—neither angels nor
beasts—even the best things of this world can never
fully satisfy us.

The writer of Ecclesiastes spent a lifetime grappling
with this confusing paradox. One by one, he examines
the things that people turn to for meaning in life: fame,
fortune, work and pleasure. And for each he reaches the
same conclusion—it's like trying to grab hold of fog.

> I have seen all the things that are done under the
> sun; all of them are meaningless, a chasing after
> the wind.   *Ecclesiastes 1 v 14*

It's not that they lack any value—he repeatedly empha-
sizes the value of a good day's work (eg: Ecclesiastes 3
v 22). It's just that our mortality—the fact that we will
all die—seems to rob everything of its value. So he con-
cludes that true wisdom can only be found in a life of
dependence on our Creator (Ecclesiastes 12 v 1-7), and
of trusting him for what lies beyond:

He has made everything beautiful in its time. He has also set eternity in the human heart; yet no one can fathom what God has done from beginning to end.   *Ecclesiastes 3 v 11*

C. S. Lewis understood this perfectly.

Creatures are not born with desires unless satisfaction for those desires exists. A baby feels hunger: well, there is such a thing as food. A duckling wants to swim: well, there is such a thing as water. Men feel sexual desire: well, there is such a thing as sex. If I find in myself a desire which no experience in this world can satisfy, the most probable explanation is that I was made for another world.
                                        Mere Christianity

So we should not be surprised by the many frustrations of this life. Rather, we should see them as a sign of, and a hunger for, another world.

God made each one of us valuable:
SO no one is disposable

After the great tragedy of humanity's fall (which we will return to), Genesis 4 records the second: Cain murders his brother Abel. God's response is fascinating. He is naturally appalled, declaring:

Your brother's blood cries out to me from the ground.   *Genesis 4 v 10*

Cain receives the divine punishment of being a "restless wanderer on the earth" (4 v 11). And yet, to allay Cain's fears that he himself has become a target, God gives him "a mark ... so that no one who found him would kill him" (4 v 15).

We see here that *all* life is precious—even the life of a murderer. Life is God's gift, and God alone can determine its length, as Job recognised:

> A person's days are determined; you have decreed the number of his months and have set limits he cannot exceed. *Job 14 v 5*

All Christian arguments about the sanctity of human life derive from this essential fact. God made us, as a race and as individual members of that race, and so we are each precious in his sight. Human value is derived from our createdness.

Each of us is born with extraordinary potential: physically, intellectually, creatively and morally. One of life's most unforgettable moments is when you first hold a newborn in your arms and wonder at the myriad paths that he or she could walk in life. Of course, none of us match perfectly what we have the potential to become. There is no perfect specimen. But that never stops us being fully human.

- *A criminal is still fully human, even if his behaviour is subhuman and dehumanising.*

- *A child with Down's Syndrome is fully human, even if her mental capacities are restricted.*

- *A grandfather is still fully human, even if he is bedbound and unable to feed himself.*

As is sometimes said, we are human *beings*, not human *doings*. Being human is about who we are in essence, from the first seconds of existence to the last. It is not about what we can achieve in life.

This is all well and good. But how come the sanctity of human life is even up for debate? Why isn't life safe and sound in this God-given habitat of perfection? Something has clearly gone wrong.

Why did God make us at all?

It's a good question—even King David brooded on it:

When I consider your heavens, the work of your fingers, the moon and the stars, which you have set in place, what is mankind that you are mindful of them, human beings that you care for them? *Psalm 8 v 3-4*

It's very clear from the Bible that God, unlike the "gods" of the ancient world, didn't make us because he was bored or lonely or needed us in any way (see Psalm 50 v 9-10 and John 17 v 5). He is utterly self-sufficient but never self-centred—the Trinity is the key to understanding that particular mystery. But he made us anyway, as an expression of his love (Jeremiah 31 v 3).

Everything he has made, including humanity, illustrates his glory and wonder (see Psalm 19 v 1-6). The pinnacle of that glory is seen in his grace poured out through Jesus (Ephesians 1 v 4-6)—and impossible though it is to get our heads round this, the cross was God's plan from before the creation of the universe (see Revelation 13 v 8)! In a way that we will not understand this side of eternity, our creation, and all that follows, brings eternal glory to God.

When does life start?

All human beings equally share the image of God and the fact that we are sinners does not completely destroy it. This is true of all of us—even before we are born. So God can tell Jeremiah:

Before I formed you in the womb I knew you.
Jeremiah 1 v 5

David can rejoice in the fact that God...

... created my inmost being; you knit me together in my mother's womb.
Psalm 139 v 13

In other words, God is involved even at the moment of conception.

The Bible never speaks of any moment at which someone somehow becomes human. This has profound implications for how we think about questions like abortion. Exodus 21 v 22-25 commands the same penalty for someone who causes the death of a baby in the womb as for someone who commits murder. This clearly indicates that God considers a baby in the womb to be as fully human as a full-grown adult.

Although there are rare circumstances where there is a more difficult choice to be made—for example, if the mother's life is at serious risk, or if the baby is the result of rape or abuse—Christians will always default to celebrating and choosing life, even when it involves hardship and difficulties. But because we believe in a gospel of grace, we should always be sympathetic and reassuring of God's love and forgiveness to those who have lost children in the past—for whatever reason.

Chapter 3

SAVED: *How does God see us?*

Centuries ago, the writer of Proverbs said that *"the fear of the Lord is the beginning of wisdom"*. Our problem is that we don't actually believe him.

We don't imagine that thinking and living independently of our Maker could be the worst kind of folly—quite the reverse in fact. It seems to many to be the height of sophistication. But that was the supreme goal of the snake's deception in the garden.

The command not to eat fruit from the tree of the knowledge of good and evil in Genesis 2 was not the first command. There were at least two others before it, both liberating. The first was to "be fruitful and increase in number; fill the earth and subdue it." (Genesis 1 v 28). The second was the gift of *everything else* to enjoy:

You are free to eat from any tree in the garden.

Genesis 2 v 16

Sometimes we think the command not to eat from the one tree was somehow God spoiling everything. But it was the *only* moral boundary that a supremely generous God gave his creatures. And it was given to them *out of love* to protect them, because:

... when you eat from it you will certainly die. *(v 17)*

But the snake wanted the man and woman to believe that defying God was actually in their interest. He said they would not...

... certainly die ... for God knows that when you
eat from it your eyes will be opened, and you will
be like God, knowing good and evil.   *(3 v 4-5)*

So here is the heart of the attraction: becoming God-like—breaking free from the God-given moral limitations built into our creation. We seize the right to determine what is good and evil—after all, who actually likes being told what to do? Even when the regulations are in our best interests, like standing behind the yellow line on the train platform, or not drink-driving.

This is far more serious than rejecting the authority of a parliament or president. They have authority over a society in so far as they are elected. But they must all obey the laws they pass since no leader can be above the law. More importantly, no one would suggest that when a citizen breaks those laws, its legislators would take this as a personal affront.

But rejecting God's rule *is* personal. It spurns his good,

generous and gracious providence for us. Even worse, it snubs the One on whom we depend for every breath. It is like a diver hating her scuba gear and imagining she can swim indefinitely without it. It might be possible for a minute or two—but eventually, the need for air will become unbearable. So it is with God—we imagine we can survive and even thrive without him. After all, Adam and Eve didn't immediately die upon eating the fruit...

But death *did* come into the world—as Abel's murder and Genesis 5's relentless drumbeat of death proves. The snake was proved wrong again and again and again. We do not thrive without God. This why King David made this sweeping, and at first sight unfair, statement:

> The fool says in his heart, "There is no God." They are corrupt, their deeds are vile; there is no one who does good.　　　　　*Psalm 14 v 1*

The point is not that people who reject dependence on God are *always* immoral or unethical. Rather, because God is the cause of all things and source of all goodness, no word or act can ever truly be good if divorced from him, even if, strictly speaking, it constitutes something that is morally good in isolation. For this is the heart of what the Bible calls sin—a life lived in God's world without gratitude to or dependence on God. This is the heart of the tragedy that has played out from that fateful day in Eden, and we see its effects within ourselves, our families, our communities and world on a daily basis.

1. Facts of life: *things go wrong*

We have quite a high opinion of ourselves on the whole. We make our plans for the future— we even call it "foreseeable", as if we really could forsee it. But still things go wrong. Best intentions are never enough. We can never understand enough, predict enough or do enough to prevent accidents or mistakes. "The best-laid plans of mice and men" are always thwarted.

If that happens even when we're at our best, what of our worst? Overthrowing divine authority prompts us to resent *any* authority. We each want to be top dog, whether over our siblings, spouse, colleagues, or rivals. This will inevitably lead to abusing those who stand in our way. And what's true for our personal relationships is true for international, diplomatic relationships.

Our limitations and flaws will lead to disaster eventually. No wonder the psalm writer sings of God looking down on the schemes and conspiracies of human affairs with wry scorn:

> The One enthroned in heaven laughs; the LORD scoffs at them. He rebukes them in his anger.
>
> *Psalm 2 v 4-5*

2. Facts of life: *things have consequences*

Whether we like it or not, God is still God. And because this is a moral universe, wrongdoing always ultimately has consequences. Just as certain lifestyles increase our susceptibility to particular diseases, so sin leads to terrible consequences. Yet, this is precisely how God wired the universe.

The apostle Paul echoes Proverbs to diagnose sin:

"Although they claimed to be wise, they became fools"
(Romans 1 v 22).

So what is God's response? Shockingly, he decides *not* to intervene.

> Therefore God gave them over in the sinful desires of their hearts to sexual impurity for the degrading of their bodies with one another. They exchanged the truth about God for a lie, and worshipped and served created things rather than the Creator.
>
> *Romans 1 v 24-25*

Here Paul identifies the enslaving noose of sexual immorality—but he could equally have referred to any human activity that constrains and controls us.

This is not God's last word on the matter. A day of justice will come—a day that our world is actually crying out for after so often being overwhelmed by injustice and cruelty. The fact that it has not yet come, and that the perpetrators of injustice keep getting away with it, is no grounds for false confidence, since he has "left the sins committed beforehand unpunished." (Romans 3 v 25; compare with Psalm 73 v 12-17). It is just a matter of time before "every mouth may be silenced and the whole world held accountable to God" (Romans 3 v 19).

King David knew that sin was no theory, though. His conscience plagued his deepest thoughts.

> When I kept silent, my bones wasted away through my groaning all day long. For day and night your hand was heavy on me.   *Psalm 32 v 3-4*

What hope is there then? See what happened when David prayed about it.

> Then I acknowledged my sin to you and did not cover up my iniquity. I said, "I will confess my transgressions to the LORD." And you forgave the guilt of my sin. *Psalm 32 v 5*

One question remains, though. How is such forgiveness possible?

3. Facts of life: *hope for rescue*

Returning to Romans, notice Paul's careful argument:

> You see, at just the right time, when we were still powerless, Christ died for the ungodly. Very rarely will anyone die for a righteous person, though for a good person someone might possibly dare to die. But God demonstrates his own love for us in this: while we were still sinners, Christ died for us. *Romans 5 v 6-8*

If you divorce yourself from the Lord of life, life eventually becomes unliveable—like the diver dispensing with the scuba gear. Death is the inevitable consequence. But it's also the *just* consequence. God has created a moral universe and he will always act with justice. We are in real danger. But as David discovered, God is both just *and* merciful. He forgives his creatures, even for rejecting him, when they return to him.

Paul explains how that's possible. It entails a death—

one death in place of another. Jesus's death on the cross. Paul's illustration shows just how astonishing that is.

History is full of great leaders and martyrs to causes. People do die for others—but only if they believe in them. But Jesus died for those who *hated and rejected* God. Such is the extent of his love. More to the point of this book, such is the value of human beings.

That only makes sense if we start with our creatures made by a loving Creator. Why else would God bother about us? It is precisely because God knit us together in our mother's womb that we matter to him—so much so that he is prepared to make the ultimate sacrifice on our behalf. This was the price for restoring us to the relationship with God that we were created for.

This is the final piece of the puzzle of human value. We have infinite worth because we are both created *and* rescued. It's irrelevant how able or disabled we are; how apparently moral or evil we are; how bright or dull, rich or poor, beautiful or ugly. None of these matter in the end—only that we are loved by the God who made and rescued us:

While we were still sinners, Christ died for us. *(v 8)*

And if God treats each individual human being like that, who are we to disparage or belittle, to oppress or enslave, to torture or to kill anyone? We might be a hybrid species, neither angels nor animals. But human beings have unique dignity and value in God's cosmos.

The creation established that. The cross demonstrated that. *For all eternity.*

When did I become a sinner?

All of us are born east of Eden—each of us inherits the inclination to reject God, and there is nothing we can do about it—it is as integral to us as our chromosomes. Our default setting is to veer away from God, not towards him. So David confesses his sin to God in startling terms:

Surely I was sinful at birth, sinful from the time my mother conceived me. *Psalm 51 v 5*

That seems a scandalous suggestion to many people—especially when you see the sheer helplessness (not to mention cuteness) of newborn babies. How on earth can they be blamed or responsible for anything, let alone this so-called "original sin"?

As a parent of teenagers, a couple of things strike me. It's amazing how early some of their (now) obviously identifiable character traits began to show themselves. So much of who they are was already present, just waiting to emerge. It's also the case that we never had to teach them how to be disobedient or naughty. It just seemed to come naturally. So while the idea of original sin is mysterious, it does seem to fit with reality.

Some people ask: "But if our sin is inherited, how can we be held responsible—it's not our fault!" But don't we all actually *want* to repeat the sin of Adam? Don't we all crave independence from God? And, without the dignity of being held accountable for our actions, we could never take credit for the things we do well.

God knows what we're like of course—and is still bothered with us. After all, that's precisely why Jesus came among us to die. As John Calvin said: "Christ is much more powerful to save than Adam was to ruin".

Chapter 4

Mirror image:
How should we see ourselves?

"I just don't know who I am anymore! One minute I feel I'm one thing; the next, it's like I'm a completely different person. It doesn't make sense!"

It's the classic cry of the hormonal teenager. But grown adults feel it too. Perhaps it always has been, but identity seems more of an issue now than ever.

Just think of the impact of the internet. The anonymity of the screen enables us to "enjoy" multiple identities, each with its own avatar, hobbies and characteristics. Even within a single browser, I can simultaneously experiment with a different gender, sexuality or ethnicity. As Peter Steiner's famous 1993 *New Yorker* cartoon put it: "On the internet, nobody knows you're a dog".

But are we that malleable? Is who we are simply a matter of what we choose to be? Sometimes it feels like it. At other times, we feel trapped in something we don't want to be. No wonder people head off to the Himalayas to "find themselves", or get addicted to extreme sports or alcohol to "lose themselves".

But having accepted God's creation as our starting point, we discover that our astonishing potential and diversity can only truly flourish within divinely given boundaries and safeguards. As a species, we have almost infinite variety, but that does not make us infinitely plastic. But we will only appreciate why this is not a problem once we get our potential and our limitations clear.

1. We're complex but integrated

A lawyer challenged Jesus to name the Old Testament's most important laws. He hardly needed a moment's thought.

The most important one is this:

> Hear, O Israel: the Lord our God, the Lord is one.
> Love the Lord your God with all your heart and with all your soul and with all your mind and with all your strength.
>
> *Mark 12 v 29-30 quoting Deuteronomy 6 v 4-5*

Jesus was clear because the Old Testament was clear. God is uniquely deserving of our total allegiance because he is our only Creator. That is why this command is the foundation of all morality. The basic point is simple: loving God concerns every aspect of a disciple's life and existence.

The intriguing thing is that Jesus made a tiny amendment. To Deuteronomy's "heart, soul and strength", he added "all your mind". There are a number of probable reasons for this. Most likely he wanted to be explicit about what an old-covenant believer would have assumed from the word "heart". That word included what we would now call the mind. But Jesus' clarification does throw light on our different components as human beings.

The words' meanings overlap, but we can summarise them like this:

- **Heart** *points to our **emotions***.

- **Mind** *points to our **intelligence***.

- **Strength** *points to our **will**,
  and perhaps our **physicality** as well.*

- **Soul** *points to our **spiritual nature***.

There is no "nothing buttery" here. Jesus points to everything that makes us human. More importantly, he is clear that each component is necessary for our Creator's worship. God is not concerned merely with the "spiritual", as if our emotions and intellects can go their separate ways. Jesus expects our devotion to God to be integrated, because we were created to be integrated.

But what of our bodies? Some Christians historically have ignored the physical world as if it was somehow unspiritual, or somehow unclean. They actually seemed embarrassed by the peculiar experience of having bodies. And let's face it, our bodies can be embarrassing. Even at peak condition and in physical perfection—not something I've ever had to deal with—we know it can't last. And even at our best, everyone has enough bodily functions to make us blush!

Yet this is how God made us. Flesh and bones were

no divine afterthought—as if God suddenly needed to devise a physical frame in which to house our minds and souls (like *Dr Who's* Daleks). Remember our creation. It was before the fall that we were made male and female—with all the emotional, spiritual and physical implications of that. This is one of the reasons why Paul describes our devotion to God like this:

> Therefore, I urge you, brothers and sisters, in view of God's mercy, to offer your bodies as a living sacrifice, holy and pleasing to God—this is your true and proper worship. *Romans 12 v 1*

Worship has become a contentious word in some circles. That's a great shame but it probably reveals our tendency to "nothing buttery" again. Some effectively reduce worship to the weekly hour we gather as a church, or even to just the few minutes of corporate singing. Others imply it can only refer to everything *except* that time! Yet neither can be right.

The word simply means "the acknowledgement of someone's worth". The God who created everything we are and have is worthy of receiving everything we are and have. That means we "love" him with every part of us.

So there should be no limits to our worship. We offer him: our thinking, our singing, our speaking, our walking, our shopping, our working, our comforting, our listening, our reproducing, our nurturing, our writing, our web-browsing, our competing, our contributing, our loving, our living. We worship with body, mind, spirit, emotions because this is what we were made for. In fact, we thrive and flourish when we live like this for God.

This is what the Bible means when it talks about *shalom*. That ancient Hebrew word is usually translated "peace"—but it means so much more. It is not just the absence of war or hatred, but is much more positive. It describes wholeness and health, with everything working well, in its right place. We could even say that *shalom* is the integration that human beings were made to enjoy.

Isn't this why a twelve-hours-a-day desk job can seriously damage physical health—even if we're only sitting? Or why an emotional trauma can have physical repercussions? Conversely, sustained physical exertion or hunger will have a negative emotional impact. A series of sleepless nights (as when a new baby arrives) makes it almost impossible to keep even minor setbacks in perspective. Most worryingly of all, our moral behaviour can have repercussions for our physical and mental wellbeing—this was David's experience in Psalm 32 (which we considered in Chapter 3).

We were created to be integrated: body, mind, emotions and spirit. So why do we imagine we will remain unaffected when things get out of sync? But that's one of the tragedies of sin. When we are out of sync with God, we get out of sync with ourselves.

2. We're finite and temporary

It doesn't matter how grand or powerful or famous I am, being human will always be frustrating.

I might command armies or write symphonies or win

a record number of Oscars, but I must still eat, sleep, wash and use the toilet. Britain's first woman Prime Minister, Margaret Thatcher, famously needed only four hours sleep a night, and many do have unusual capacities like that. But she still needed *some* sleep. We can all still trip over shoelaces, or vomit after eating a dodgy curry, or endure sadness. No one is immune from the limitations of earthbound life.

This is where we are so different from God. We all share the same physical, earthbound constraints.

- *We can't breathe under water but we can't survive* without *water*.
- *We can't be in two places at once.*
- *We can't achieve everything we want.*
- *We get easily distracted and our energy levels always flag.*
- *We can't know everything, and what we do know is always provisional to some extent.*

We should be clear that these limitations do not compromise God's image in us. They are simply come with the territory of being embodied, being human. The issue is how we handle that. Will it lead us to put trust in the One without these limitations?

Of course, our greatest limitation is perhaps our lifespan. Paul describes how we are "wasting away", with "momentary troubles" in this life before we return to the dust we were made with (see 2 Corinthians 4 v 16 and Psalm 90 v 3). Our eyes and ears gradually fail, our organs tire and bits seem to start falling off. Nobody actually dies of old age. Diseases will do for us all in the end, if calamity or criminality doesn't get us first!

This isn't how it was supposed to be. In Eden, Adam and Eve could eat fruit from the tree of life. But their rejection of the life-giving Creator made death both a just and inevitable consequence that has been inherited by all humans—what Paul calls "the wages of sin" (Romans 6 v 23). So die we shall.

In our teens or twenties, we don't generally give much thought to our built-in mortality. We may be vaguely aware that we are all waiting in line at the cemetery gates, but few feel the weight of our mortality. Death happens to other people, to older people. When it happens to our peers, we're traumatised. But it is an inescapable fact of human life.

At our birth, we enter a world of wonder but also of grief. We just never know how much wonder or grief we will experience. Or when. That's why one essential task for Christian preachers and pastors is to help people face their mortality (in a pastorally sensitive way of course!) before it comes their way.

All of this should make us get real about two important truths.

We shouldn't expect to "go it alone"

My gifts and limitations were always meant to be complemented by others' different gifts and limitations. It's one reason why New Testament church leadership was always plural. Churches led by individuals who are surrounded by clones are unhealthy. God gave us diversity because he wanted us to be interdependent.

Isolating myself from others in the hope that I'll never need to lean on someone else is actually quite dangerous. We were created to be social ("It is not good for the man to be alone", Genesis 2 v 18), and we thrive best with friends and family even when they might have difficult things to say. "Wounds from a friend can be trusted, but an enemy multiplies kisses" (Proverbs 27 v 6).

We shouldn't expect too much of others

Adulation of celebrities, athletes or even pastors is always doomed. Why should gifting in one area of life guarantee it in all areas? Even the best are still limited. And all end up in the same place. Yet, somehow, we still manage to be surprised when a celebrity goes off the edge, or a pastor turns out to have been hiding some dark secret for years. The Bible is much more realistic:

> Hopes placed in mortals die with them; all the promise of their power comes to nothing.
>
> *Proverbs 11 v 7*

Two friends stood at the graveside of a wealthy US oil magnate. One asked: "So how much did he leave?" "He left everything," came the reply.

This is no recipe for despair though. It is simply another reason for seeing why the gospel is such great news. We were made ultimately for a relationship with our Creator—because he is unlimited and eternal. When he makes promises, they definitely do not come to nothing.

3. We're disintegrating and conflicted

When God does anything, he does it brilliantly. Consider the verdict after the cosmos was complete. It was "good" and "very good" (Genesis 1). And that included us! There were no design flaws in human beings. With a far greater attention to detail than an Apple iPhone or a mediaeval cathedral, we were formed to have the perfect integration of body, mind and soul.

Yet that's obviously not our experience now. Not only do we wear out over time—parts of our body gradually stop doing what we want them to do—but we can't seem to hold ourselves together. We confuse ourselves, let alone our friends, with our inconsistencies and flaws. Paul knew all about this.

> I do not understand what I do. For what I want to do I do not do, but what I hate I do. And if I do what I do not want to do, I agree that the law is good. As it is, it is no longer I myself who do it, but it is sin living in me. *Romans 7 v 15-17*

We can all relate to this, and yet it's so unsettling: as if rival factions are slogging it out inside our heads. It's a tussle between duty and desire, between what we want and what we ought to do. Why is this?

On one hand **sin is deceptive**, conning us into believing that what we want to do is beneficial for us (or if not beneficial exactly, then inconsequential). It tricks us into doubting the goodness of God's gift of moral boundaries. That has a disintegrating effect: it robs people of self-awareness like a drunk driver who never looks in the rear-view mirror, and it causes that weirdest of cancers: *self-deception*. As Jeremiah warned:

> The heart is deceitful above all things and beyond cure. Who can understand it? *Jeremiah 17 v 9*

On the other hand **sin is destructive**. Sin *always* spoils and dismantles. It will always break up what God has joined together. That won't necessarily happen immediately, but we reap what we sow. For "whoever sows to please their flesh, from the flesh will reap destruction" (Galatians 6 v 7-8). "Flesh" here simply means the strength of our selfish desires (wherever they lead us). We can see sin's destructiveness in the detrimental effect our sin has on our own stability and wellbeing.

This is inevitable when we "divorce" ourselves from God. That will always cause disharmony and disintegration. It might be hard to accept, but it's certainly hard to deny. The wonder is that this is far from the last word on human experience...

4. But we're resurrected and growing

Paul continued his gardening illustration about sowing seeds like this: "Whoever sows to please the Spirit, from the Spirit will reap eternal life" (Galatians 6 v 8). The point is simple. There is an alternative to our fleshly passions. Rely on the Spirit to lead us through. But perhaps this sounds a bit tenuous, as if it is just a matter of choosing to resist the wrong path at every fork in the road? The problem of course is that if things were left to us, we would undoubtedly choose the flesh over God's Spirit every time.

The good news is that Paul's appeal comes in the context of what God has already guaranteed; because God actually started the work of restoration and integration in us, at the very moment we first bowed the knee to Christ. Paul simply wants to emphasise the responsibilities that come with this. Check out this little list of confidence-boosters!

- **Conversion:** Nobody can come to Christ without the Spirit, because it is the most counter-intuitive thing that someone who has tried to live life without God can do. *I want you to know that no one who is speaking by the Spirit of God says, "Jesus be cursed," and no one can say, "Jesus is Lord," except by the Holy Spirit (1 Corinthians 12 v 3).*

- **Resurrection:** Forgiveness and being restored to friendship with God are just the start when it comes to Christ's victory. In Romans 8 Paul tells us that God's Spirit takes up residence in us. The new life he brings is nothing less than a personal resurrection! *"If the Spirit of him who raised Jesus from the dead is living in you, he who raised Christ from the dead will also give life to your mortal bodies because of his Spirit who lives in you" (Romans 8 v 11).*

- **Guarantee:** The Spirit's residency is permanent. As a result, we can know that the future is guaranteed. When a farmer gets a taste of the "firstfruits", it is the first indication of the quality of the harvest to come. So it is with coming to know God. We are placed squarely on the road to total rescue. *"[We], who have the firstfruits of the Spirit, groan inwardly as we wait eagerly for our adoption to sonship, the redemption of our bodies. For in this hope we were saved"* (Romans 8 v 23-24).

I don't know anyone who relishes waiting. It's not just children in the back seat who moan, whinge and intone that infuriating mantra: "Are we there yet?" But waiting is a fact of life, and it is particularly a fact of the Christian life. What God has started, he will finish (see Philippians 1 v 6), but his timetable is nearly always different from our own. It is a matter of working out what we already have, and what we must wait for.

For our purposes here, Christians have already received God's Spirit, who guarantees the future—and that means the full experience of God's adoption and bodily redemption or rescue.

But take note: Paul is not implying that our adoption and redemption are only future experiences—he has already said that the Spirit has brought about our adoption (Romans 8 v 15), and that Christ has redeemed us (Galatians 3 v 13, Romans 3 v 24). He's simply stating that the end result will be a complete and thorough restoration to what we were created to be: body, heart, mind and soul, integrated and harmonious, restored into a new society and created order, all because of Jesus.

I'll never forget Pat, who was a stalwart member of the first church I ever worked in. She had some wretched crippling illness a bit like brittle bone disease, but somehow worse than that. For years, her life had been lived on the edge, even though she never went very far from her home, because the smallest stumble could be excruciating or even fatal. She had to go everywhere with her body covered in splints, like a kind of exoskeleton, seated in a motorised wheelchair.

Her physical frailty profoundly affected her emotional wellbeing and her spiritual priorities, as you would expect. But her remarkable trust in the Lord's goodness shone out whenever I met her. She was an inspiration.

The thing I most remember though was her saying with glistening eyes:

"I just can't wait for my new body, Mark. It's going to be so wonderful."

It's obvious why she was so desperate. I can't imagine how hard it must be to keep battling one's sin when having to endure chronic pain.

But it doesn't matter where our own particular pains or temptations or frailties lie. The promise of the gospel is that, because of Christ, we can be fully restored, healed and integrated. Everything will be in sync; we won't be torn in different directions; we won't be conned by sin's empty promises. Everything will be in proper working order, restored to our manufacturer's settings!

I don't know how that prospect makes you feel. Relief for one thing, I expect. But a longing, and even a groaning, while we wait, more likely.

What a great day it will be!

What is a soul?

The Bible does teach that there is a distinction between our bodies and souls—and while it is possible for them to be separated (for example, when a believer dies and the soul awaits the bodily resurrection), they were never meant to be. The ancient Greeks believed that the spiritual world was superior to the physical, and so despised the body. Sadly, this view infected the thinking of the church, so that it is quite common for Christians, wrongly, to think of eternity as a purely "spiritual" existence in heaven.

This view is entirely incompatible with the Bible. The physical realm is a crucial part of God's good creation (Genesis 1 v 31 and 1 Timothy 4 v 4-5). More to the point, Jesus' resurrection proves that our bodies will be rescued eternally with him (1 Corinthians 15 v 42-44). God intended us to have bodies and they are an intrinsic part of what it means to be human. For all its limitations, the body is not something to escape from, but to rejoice in.

But what precisely am I made up of as a human being? Christians have differed on how to understand what the Bible teaches on this question.

- Some have argued that we are made as integrated physical beings, so there is no way we can speak meaningfully about an existence without a body. So when we die, we will have no consciousness until we are united with our resurrection body. This view is called "soul sleep". Although this may be philosophically convincing, it ignores clear references like Jesus' words to the thief on the cross: "Today you will be with me in paradise" (Luke 23 v 43).

- Others argue that we are made of three parts: body, soul and spirit (1 Thessalonians 5 v 23): the soul being the "essential me" and our spirit being the part of me that relates to God. Critics of this view suggest that this wording is not a list of "parts" but a way of summing up the whole person.

- Most, however, default to thinking of there being two united, interconnected parts—a body and a soul—the soul being the part that incorporates everything that makes me "me".

The situation is complicated because the original words used are often translated differently, and are themselves picture language. So the word most often translated "spirit" (Greek: *psyche*), and the word translated "soul" (Greek: *pneuma*) are both words derived from "breath", "wind" or "air". Their use recalls the creation, where man was made from the dust of the ground, and then God "breathed into his nostrils the breath of life" (Genesis 2 v 7).

The Bible writers also seem to use these two words interchangeably, as when Mary sings: *"My soul glorifies the Lord; and my spirit rejoices in God my Saviour"* (Luke 1 v 46-47)—a poetic way of repeating the same idea.

What matters most, perhaps, is that we are made to be integrated beings—dust and breath—and that when our bodies return to dust, Christians can be confident that they will be cared for and kept safe by God as we wait to be united with a new resurrection body fit for eternity in the new creation.

But don't I have to express myself to be properly human?

The cry of our age is: "I cannot be fully human unless I am allowed to express myself fully. My ideas, feelings, sexuality, rage, poems, etc". Repressing "who I am" is bad. Having the freedom to express who I am is good.

Of course, much of this is good. We live in a culture of choice and freedom which has given wonderful opportunities for education, life choices and artistic expression. But there is a flaw when this view ignores our fallenness. Our hearts might cry out for many things, and we can *feel* unfulfilled until they are met; but our hearts are also idol factories, and the source of all kinds of evil thoughts and desires. What may *feel* right, may be plain wrong. Christians will always look to the Maker's instructions for clarity about our deceitful hearts. Our loving God has given us boundaries to show what will lead to our liberty and flourishing. As in Eden, it is the law of the Lord that offers perfect freedom (see James 1 v 25).

For Christians, who know we are created to "be fruitful and multiply", singleness or childlessness can be troubling. Am I less than I should be if I am alone, or if we cannot have children for whatever reason? These are deeply felt issues for many, often not helped by couples who refer (wrongly) to each other as "my other half", or who give any sense of superiority because of their fertility. We should remember that Jesus was both single and childless, and was the perfect expression of humanity. We are and can be complete and fully human in and of ourselves, because our humanity rests chiefly on our relationship with God, not on the temporary states of marriage or parenthood.

Chapter 5

Islands or continents: *How can we live together?*

'll never forget watching the second plane career into the Twin Towers live on TV—and the fact that when I drove into downtown Kampala later that afternoon, there were police checkpoints everywhere. It was an indication of the speed of the world's news media, and also the deep interconnectedness of international affairs. After all, *Al Qaeda* had been behind the US Embassy bombings in Dar Es Salaam and Nairobi, so the reaction of Uganda's security forces was not as irrational as it might have first looked.

Still, the news took time to reach remoter parts of Kenya. The Masai village of Enoosaen had no radio or TV, so they only heard about the attack ten months later in June 2002, when 25-year-old Kimeli Naiyomah returned from studying in the United States.

Skyscrapers were inconceivable to the villagers of course, and they'd never heard of *Al Qaeda*. But the community was deeply affected when it heard how "bad people" had started fires in buildings so high that when people jumped out, instant death was the certain outcome. After some discussion, the elders decided that they would donate their most prized gifts to the victims' families: 14 cows.

At a ceremony that would have "made the toughest cynic weep", a senior US diplomat was formally handed the cattle and urged to take them back to New York. This was obviously an awkward and impractical suggestion. But they did agree on selling the animals to buy Masai jewellery, which could then be given to the families.

It was an astonishing act of selfless compassion. Their offer to assist in hunting down Bin Laden was perhaps less welcome, but perfectly understandable in those who wanted to stand in solidarity.

Remembering our humanity:
what we were made to share

Because the world is so divided (on ethnic, ideological, or economic grounds), it is frighteningly easy to over-look everything human beings share. We focus so much energy on patrolling the boundaries of our cliques with that age-old propagandist's weapon of demonising out-siders. Insiders consequently want nothing to do with them. That is just as well, because if they did fraternise with "the enemy", they might just realise they're not so bad after all. They're even "just like us".

Human beings are simultaneously connected and frag-mented. We are united by our common createdness. Every one of us is made in God's image—a fact worth bearing in mind whenever we meet someone new. But we are equally affected by our common defiance of God. Immersed as he was in the Jewish Scriptures, it's no surprise that Jesus was profoundly conscious of both realities.

So when Jesus was pressed by a lawyer to name the most important commandment, he actually named two. After the command to love God, he says:

> The second is this: "Love your neighbour as yourself." There is no commandment greater than these. *Mark 12 v 31*

Love for our neighbour is to be as all-encompassing as love for God. It is to be with body, heart, mind and soul. It is also to reflect God's love for us. That means this love is to be as indiscriminate as God's love—a love available to all who are made in the same image.

Religious people have often struggled with that. We tend to avoid the less morally upright. But Jesus was blunt. In Luke 10, another lawyer tests Jesus, but finds himself on the receiving end of the questions. He answers Jesus in the same way, with that two-part summary of the law. He naturally assumed that there should be boundaries to who qualifies as a neighbour—which would make the law easier to obey. Jesus's response is astounding: his parable of the Good Samaritan. A man loves a complete stranger in the most practical but sacrificial way imaginable—rescuing, caring and giving. He donates several days' wages for his upkeep, with the option for more if required. Jesus then tells the lawyer to do exactly the same—for any of his neighbours.

What Jesus is saying is that to be truly human—to fulfil the potential of God's image in us—we need to love other people with the same commitment and passion. If that seems way too difficult, remember this; it's how we were created to live. Which means it's the best way to live: in a society knitted together by sacrificial love.

We are not to be inaccessible islands isolated by oceans, but individual countries linked together on a continental landmass. This is as central to being human as anything else we've considered. It's an advantage that African culture (at its best) has on the west. It avoids the social apartheid of the solitary nuclear family with 2.4 kids, or the tiny network of work colleagues.

If it takes a village to raise a child, it takes participation in society to properly express being human.

This makes perfect sense for people made in God's image. As the apostle John plainly tells us:

God is love.   *1 John 4 v 8, 16*

That simple statement would be a sheer impossibility if God was not *Trinity*. If God was just "one", he could never be "love"; for before the creation of the cosmos, he wouldn't have anything or anyone to love apart from himself. That would be a flat contradiction of his nature: self-love is the opposite of genuine love. Genuine love is the giving of oneself to and for another —as the good Samaritan did for the naked stranger in the ditch. That's why Jesus declared that:

Greater love has no one than this: to lay down
one's life for one's friends.   *John 15 v 13*

But because God *is* Trinity—three distinguishable Persons bound by the joy of eternal self-giving—relationships are essential to who God is. No wonder the only "not good" thing in the creation story was human loneliness. Being created in the image of a trinitarian God means we will most likely flourish in relationships with others. And that will be true even for us introverts!

The Bible unpacks this in four distinct ways:

1. We are made and saved:
to live in interdependent community

One common anxiety people have about joining a church is that it somehow robs people of their personalities. We're scared we might get turned into clones or else judged for being different.

That's quite ironic these days. Advertisers seduce consumers with the allure of rebellious freedom, but still produce an entire generation with jeans ripped in the same places and tweeting on phones in the same limited range of colours. Visit any high street on a Saturday afternoon, and you'll see more evidence of conformity than you are likely to find in many churches.

Still, it's not an entirely unjustified fear. Church leaders with strong characters too easily impress an unhelpful mould on people, weeding out or putting off difference and dissent. Then those that do stay can sometimes even begin to pick up their pastor's mannerisms. But this is not how church life is meant to be.

Of course, getting this right is tricky. But as individuals, each with a unique blend of personality, gifting and experience, we all need each other. In fact, it's only in relationship with others that we can truly exercise our gifts.

It's one reason why the New Testament describes the church as a body—the body of Christ. It was always God's purpose to create a diversified church, as varied as the human race itself. After all, his goal is nothing less than the rescue of the first creation into a new creation. That's why it is to be drawn from men and women of every social and racial background conceivable. Christ's blood "purchased for God persons from every tribe and language and people and nation" (Revelation 5 v 9). God is emphatically *not* to be identified with only one nationality or language in the new creation.

As we have seen, human beings are complicated, and that's just on the physical level. Paul uses that simple fact to illustrate how each body part belongs to the whole, regardless of its attractiveness or visibility. No part can say: "I do not belong" because "there are many parts, but one body" (1 Corinthians 12 v 15-19).

No part can say to another: "I don't need you!" because "God has put the body together" (1 Corinthians 12 v 21-24). Our differences should not be obstacles but assets! The sum is greater than the parts.

Paul's specific challenge is for churches to give particular attention to those who would otherwise be less valued or honoured. It's scandalous when a society's prejudices are replicated in church life, as was the case among the Christians in ancient Corinth.

There should be no division in the body, but ... its parts should have equal concern for each other. If

one part suffers, every part suffers with it; if one
part is honoured, every part rejoices with it.

1 Corinthians 12 v 25-26

We were made to belong to something greater than
ourselves. Of course, some relationships will be closer;
some will be longer lasting. They might shift and vary
at different stages of life. We operate within a series of
concentric circles of relationship (from close family out
to acquaintances).

But we do need others. For if love is the summary of
the law, we need people to love! The spin-off is that we
also have people who love us. These are people who will
weep with us and laugh with us, suffer with us and persevere with us. No wonder the writer of Hebrews urged
his readers not to "give up meeting as some are in the
habit of doing", but to persevere in encouraging one
another by gathering together (Hebrews 10 v 25).

This need for others is not a sign of weakness. It's not
some consequence of the fall, as if we were originally
made for self-sufficiency. It is true that many feel driven
to that because of bad experiences with others. Their
fingers have been burned once too often and so trust is
too great a risk. Tragically this is a story too often told of
church fellowships.

Yet that's not the way it's meant to be, as C.S. Lewis
grasped:

To love at all is to be vulnerable. Love anything,
and your heart will certainly be wrung and possibly
be broken. If you want to make sure of keeping

it intact, you must give your heart to no one, not even to an animal. Wrap it carefully round with hobbies and little luxuries; avoid all entangle-ments; lock it up safe in the casket or coffin of your selfishness. But in that casket—safe, dark, motionless, airless—it will change. It will not be broken; it will become unbreakable, impenetrable, irredeemable … The only place outside Heaven where you can be perfectly safe from all the dan-gers … of love is Hell.   *The Four Loves*

We were created for interdependence, not independence. Isn't that why God made us so different? Needing others is no fault, still less a sin. It is how we were designed.

2. We are made and saved:
to be other-person centred

From our first days in kindergarten, we're coached (perhaps "conditioned" is not too strong a word) to be self-centred. We are encouraged to be strong and inde-pendent, to be "captains of our souls and masters of our fate". That's the only way to survive in this cut-throat world—it's survival of the brightest, richest, sexiest, toughest. Look at any aspect of modern life—those at the top are rarely plain "nice". Ruthlessness and ambi-tion got them there. Of course, some drop out from this culture in disgust, but it is still a norm.

But as John Ruskin put it: "When a man is wrapped up in himself, he makes a pretty small package". To assume that life is just a matter of winning by "dying with the most toys", as an old bumper sticker put it, is to shrug off so many aspects of our divine image. Even worse, it invariably entails harming or destroying others. That is hinted at by this anonymous poem, entitled: *The Child's Law of Adverse Possession*.

If I like it, it's mine.
If it's in my hand, it's mine.
If I can take it from you, it's mine.
If I had it a little while ago, it's mine.
If it's mine,
    it must never appear to be yours in any way.
If I'm doing or building something,
    all the pieces are mine.
If it looks just like mine, it is mine.
If I saw it first, it's mine.
If you are playing with something and put it down,
it automatically becomes mine.

                    If it's broken, it's yours.

It's not just children who function like that. Yet isn't it interesting that we expect more of grown-ups? For one mark of maturity is growing out of this self-centredness. That's increasingly tough in a culture that wages a winning battle to appeal to our self-centredness with its slogans: *Just Do It*, *Obey your thirst*, and *Because you're worth it*.

There is a different way. But it is quite shocking today. In his letter to the Philippians, Paul said this:

Do *nothing* out of selfish ambition or vain conceit. Rather, in humility value others above yourselves, not looking to your own interests but each of you to the interests of the others. *Philippians 2 v 3-4*

That's hardly the advice people get at Harvard Business School or if running for public office. It seems absurd, and even dangerous if some psychologists are to be believed. Yet Paul is insistent. His argument is derived from the heart of Christianity: Jesus himself.

The extraordinary poem in Philippians chapter 2 traces Christ's unique journey, starting in eternity and returning to eternity, via the most appalling humiliation and suffering.

> In your relationships with one another, have the
> same mindset as Christ Jesus:
> Who, being in very nature God,
>> did not consider equality with God something
>> to be used to his own advantage;
> rather, he made himself nothing
>> by taking the very nature of a servant,
>> being made in human likeness.
> And being found in appearance as a man,
>> he humbled himself
>> by becoming obedient to death—
>> even death on a cross!
> Therefore God exalted him to the highest place
>> and gave him the name that is above
>> every name,
> that at the name of Jesus every knee should bow,
>> in heaven and on earth and under the earth,
>> and every tongue acknowledge that Jesus
>> Christ is Lord,
>> to the glory of God the Father.   *(v 5-11)*

Jesus the Creator was never too proud to become Jesus the Creature. But his descent didn't end there. He surrendered not to the social status of a king, but of a slave. He was even prepared to "become obedient to death, even death on a cross" (Philippians 2 v 8). Do you see the significance of that? Jesus renounced all his human rights, including the ultimate one: *the right to life.*

This journey's first jolt is that it's precisely what God planned—all three Persons of the Trinity were committed to it. That is why the story doesn't end in death. In response to Jesus' supreme sacrifice: "God exalted him to the highest place". This does not mean God is against human rights. The point is that there might be something greater, more inspiring—dare I say it, more important—than human rights. That is human love. For it was love that compelled Christ to go to the cross.

Then comes the second, and more unsettling, jolt. Look how Paul introduces this song: "In your relationships with one another, have the same mindset as Christ Jesus". He doesn't say: "generally resemble", "be a bit like" or "get onto Jesus's wavelength". He says: "Have the same mindset as Christ Jesus"—no ifs, no buts. That doesn't necessarily mean go and get yourself martyred, but it does mean *love as he loved.* For love is the only thing that trumps all rights.

But Paul is not advocating some sort of harsh regime of enforced self-denial. He's simply building on something that every Christian has experienced.

Follow God's example, therefore, as dearly loved

children and live a life of love, just as Christ loved
us and gave himself up for us. *Ephesians 5 v 1-2*

This isn't "love people to get God to love you". There's
no arm-twisting or bargaining involved. Instead, the
primary motivation for loving others is that *Christ loved
us first*. After experiencing that, how can we not want
others to share Christ's love?

That's the key to life together. For it is only this kind
of sacrificial love that can make church life work. I've
no evidence to back this up, but my hunch is that even
when important doctrinal issues need to be debated,
they are not necessarily the root causes of division in
churches that split or splinter. More often than not, it
is the lack of sacrificial and generous love on some or
all sides. That's certainly what was going wrong in the
Philippian church.

Yet the challenge goes deeper. Jesus's cross was for *all*,
regardless of how unlovable or unpleasant some might
be. So we have no excuse for discriminating against
anyone. Every church has its "awkward squad" of
unloveable and "hard-to-love" people. It really matters
how we treat them.

When he was leader of the church I am part of in
London, John Stott did what nearly all pastors do. He
would be available at the door as people left. When he
spotted some of the trickier customers approaching, he
would deliberately remind himself that these people
were created by God in his image, and loved by God
in Christ at his cross. So he had no excuse not to love
them too.

And he did.

He had a remarkable gift of giving his full attention to the individual he was talking to, even if far more "important" or "strategic" people filed out past him. It was a small but powerful way of putting Paul's words into practice.

3. We are made and saved:
to offer grace to all

God is a lavish and generous Giver. And he's pretty indiscriminate about it too. After all:

> He causes his sun to rise on the evil and the good, and sends rain on the righteous and the unrighteous.   *Matthew 5 v 45*

For all the mysteries of life in this world, there are still so many good things in it. That includes the people that God has created in his image—and whether they acknowledge it or not, their talents, attributes and kindness are all reflections of the One who gave them. "Every good and perfect gift is from above, coming down from the Father of the heavenly lights" (James 1 v 17). This is what some call God's common grace.

Now, a person's greatest, eternal need is to be reconciled to his or her Creator and Rescuer. How can it not be, after what Christ has done for us? Each of us has the duty and privilege of playing a part in that reconciling work. Paul explains his wanting to "persuade others" of God's holiness and grace, by saying that the "God, who reconciled us to himself ... gave us this ministry of reconciliation" (2 Corinthians 5 v 18). It can't be dry duty when love is the motivation.

> Christ's love compels us ... he died for all, that
> those who live should no longer live for themselves
> but for him who died for them and was raised
> again.   *2 Corinthians 5 v 14-15*

As we have seen, this is what we were created for: to live for the one who made us. So in brokering reconciliation with God, we are helping people to become more who they were made to be. It is a tiny, but essential, piece of the cosmic jigsaw that is God's rescue plan for his creation. For with this great *reconciliation* comes our great *restoration*. How can we not want everyone to join the crowds in the new creation?

So if we love our God and our neighbour, we will be determined evangelists of God's grace. Evangelism is an act of love from start to finish... or it should be. When genuine love is not the motivating factor, it deteriorates into something very ugly indeed: a bid for control, prestige or wealth, perhaps, but never ultimately in the interests of the individuals we are trying to reach. They have ceased to be people, and are instead targets, or even victims. The grim irony is that we merely prove we are living for ourselves, not for the one who died for us.

No wonder so many get put off the whole idea of Christianity when they see Christians behaving in this way.

There is a trend among some Christians to assume that the practical love we are to share is to be exclusively shown to fellow believers, whereas the primary way to love and serve non-believers is to share the Christian message with them. It is certainly true that the gospel needs words—images or even deeds cannot be enough. Paul made that clear:

> How can they believe in the one of whom they have not heard? And how can they hear without someone preaching to them?   *Romans 10 v 14*

Our culture devalues words—but we cannot do without them in life. We certainly can't do without them in the work of reconciliation to which God has called us all. Francis of Assisi probably never did say: "Preach the gospel—use words if you have to". But even if he had, it wouldn't have been very helpful. Paul clearly thought that words *were* necessary.

But there is a point to that old line. It is trying to counteract the notion that we communicate by just using words. But how can God's mission in his world be reduced to just words, to just evangelism, to just discipling others?

Jesus offers a fascinating example of getting this right early on in his ministry. In Mark 1, he has raised a storm of publicity with his healings, exorcisms and teaching. He then makes himself scarce in the early hours in order to pray, making his disciples hunt him down, which they do with the complaint that "everyone is looking for you!" (Mark 1 v 37). Jesus's reply is unnerving:

> Let us go somewhere else—to the nearby villages—so that I can preach there also. That is why I have come.

It's startling. But as soon as he *does* move on, he preaches of course... and continues to drive out demons. In fact Mark's very next incident is a healing of leprosy. Jesus' own priorities are not so exclusive that he stops doing other good things.

It's striking, for example, how vague Paul can be about the specifics of neighbourly love.

> For we are God's handiwork, created in Christ Jesus **to do good works**, which God prepared in advance for us to do.   *Ephesians 2 v 10*

> Let us not become weary in doing good ... as we have opportunity, let us **do good to all people**, especially to those who belong to the family of believers.   *Galatians 6 v 9-10*

Notice that reminder of practical love for Christians—presumably some in Galatia were overlooking that.

> Command them **to do good**, to be rich in **good deeds**, and to be generous and willing to share.
>   *1 Timothy 6 v 18*

> Christ ... gave himself for us to redeem us from all wickedness and to purify for himself a people that are his very own, **eager to do what is good.**
>   *Titus 2 v 14*

We are to be Christ-like in both mindset *and* lifestyle. We are to love as he loved—in whatever way is required: whether by helping a mugging victim in a ditch (like the Good Samaritan), or explaining the wonder of God's grace (as Philip did to the Ethiopian in Acts 8), or showing hospitality to strangers (Hebrews 13 v 2).

Never lose sight of our common humanity with our neighbours. We should share grace commonly, because God shared his grace commonly.

4. We are made and saved:
for responsibility for the world we inhabit

Reality TV producers are always looking for the next big thing to draw the crowds, so it was just a matter of time before they landed on environmental health officers.

These people have to enter buildings left in an appalling state because of their owners' neglect or illness. On shows like *The Life of Grime* and *Grimefighters*, viewers are supposed to be glued to their screens with grim fascination that a kitchen or bathroom could have become so obscene with so many health hazards. It's no small relief that nobody has invented TVs that can accompany sound and image with authentic smells.

How on earth can anyone live like that? Even the least house-proud tidy up every now and then, surely? And yet the truth is that many of us in the West treat our planet with this kind of exploitation and neglect, as we assume that it exists simply for our convenience. We enjoy a remarkable consumer lifestyle and assume it has no real impact on anything. What damage will one cell phone do? But we fail to see the devastation and destruction caused by the manufacture of millions of phones (through mining, energy production, pollution from waste products, and so on). Out of sight too easily means out of mind.

As we saw in chapter 2, human beings are integral to God's purposes in creation. We have a unique place within it: we are part of the created order, but distinct from it. Because we are made in God's image, we have God's mandate to rule over creation—not in exploitative domination, but in caring stewardship. We are embedded in this world with a job to do, just as Adam was originally placed in Eden and told "to work it and take care of it," literally "to serve and keep it safe" (Genesis 2 v 15). The only change is how much harder it became after the fall. Slog, sweat and tears became the order of the day, since once humanity was dislocated from God we also became dislocated from the environment we were meant for.

Our actions always have consequences. So our neglect and exploitation of the world we inhabit will too. How can they not? And the impact on human health and welfare is only going to get worse ultimately. It was not how we were made to live. It is nothing like the *shalom* that God intended for us, with everything in healthy harmony in its right place, so that every creature and every person can flourish and thrive.

If so much of what we have seen in this chapter seems an impossible ideal for human beings, we must turn now to the one person who proved that it was possible: Jesus of Nazareth, the perfect human being.

Can I lose God's image in me?

As I hope you are beginning to see, being made in God's image is a complex but wonderful reality. This is why we should avoid "nothing buttery" when discussing it. This truth—that we are made in the image of God—is the foundation for everything the Bible teaches about human beings. So imagine that this pie chart, with its various segments, illustrates all the different components of God's image in us.

Despite my sinfulness, I cannot lose it; it is integral to who I am. But each of us grows the various aspects of God's image in different ways. Our diversity means that some of us are more rational than others, some more compassionate or sociable, some more creative, some more reliable, and so on. But because of our fallenness, they are each twisted and stunted—to varying degrees of course. And because of other constraints (such as from accident or disease), various components get impaired. This means that we live out God's image unevenly. What results is something that is twisted, but the original pattern can still be seen.

This is crucial:

- I might have failed morally, but I still have value

and dignity because of God's image in me (like the murderer Cain).

- I might be an embryo where almost everything about me is a question of potential (very little has developed at all, even though the speed of growth in the womb is astonishing). But I still have value and dignity because of God's image in me.

- I might start losing my mental faculties like memory or the ability to recognise people, but I still have value and dignity because of God's image in me (like an Alzheimer's sufferer).

Of course, there was one life which showed the potential of God's Image at its fullest: Jesus. We could represent him like this. Everything about him is integrated, fully developed and perfect. More on this in Chapter 6.

The best of us: *Why did Jesus become human?*

The story is told of a little girl kept awake by a thunderstorm. She ran trembling downstairs to her mother. "Mummy, I'm scared." Her mother replied: "Darling, you're perfectly safe. God loves you and he'll take care of you.

Her daughter replied: "I know God loves me. But Mummy, when it's thundering and lightning outside, I want someone with skin on to love me."

Love can be expressed in so many different ways. Sometimes it's simply the right word people need to hear. Sometimes it's the relief of help with a difficult job. Sometimes it's just a wordless hug. We use every aspect of being human—the physical, the emotional and the mental—to prove our love. The staggering thing about God is that he does too. He became a human being. In Christ, we find a "God with skin" to love us.

This was no mirage or deception. His humanity was

no pretence. His skin wasn't a "cloaking device", as used by the aliens in the *Men in Black* movies. No, he was fully human in every way except for sin. He genuinely was *like* us because **he was one of us**. It's just that he was so much more.

The New Testament writers are clear that Jesus was both fully human and fully divine—he was both 100% divine and 100% human, not 50-50 of each. The evidence for his humanity is everywhere:

- *His family tree:* In Matthew 1 and Luke 3 we read about Jesus' human ancestors. The writers make it clear that he was human (descended from Adam); Jewish (descended from Abraham); and royal (descended from David). His willingness to identify with all humanity is reinforced by the inclusion of five women marginalised by race or reputation.

- *His physical nature:* Jesus came into the world as we all do. He passed through childhood and puberty to adulthood. Like us all, Jesus got exhausted, hungry and thirsty. If you had encountered Jesus, nothing about him would have suggested he was anything other than a Jewish man from "up north". Presumably his accent, complexion and looks made it clear that he came from Galilee (see Matthew 21 v 11). The ultimate evidence of his physicality was that his heart really did stop beating when he died on the cross (see John 19 v 30-34).

- *His intellectual abilities:* Jesus was renowned for his teaching brilliance. His ability to communicate so *well demonstrated real intellectual ability. But Luke tells us that he "grew in wisdom" (Luke 2 v 52). He knew his Bible inside out, and could think systematically and rationally—as in the Sermon on the Mount. His unforgettable stories appealed to all walks of life, and he could think on his feet and handle hostile inquisitors with ease. No surprise then that even opponents addressed him as "Good Teacher."*

■ **His emotional depths:** *Jesus was deeply affected by the people and events around him. Seeing the suffering of those he loved caused him acute pain. In fact, the most striking thing about Jesus' emotions was their intensity. His anger, grief and fear at various times were overwhelming. The worst came in Gethsemane as he braced himself for that first Good Friday.*

So far so good. *But so what?* What makes Jesus' human nature significant?

The Bible presents Jesus to us as the mediator between God and man:

> For there is one God and one mediator between God and mankind, the man Christ Jesus, who gave himself as a ransom for all people.   *1 Timothy 2 v 5-6*

Mediation in a dispute requires a third party trusted by both sides to act as a go-between. But Jesus uniquely goes further. He actually *represents* both sides simply because he *belongs* to both sides. How can someone be our "advocate with the Father" when we sin, if he is not one of us? How can we be sure of access into the presence of God, unless God himself prepares a way back to him?

Jesus' identity as both fully human and fully divine is essential for the cross to be the means of forgiveness of sins and our salvation. That's why the apostles were so concerned to oppose those who denied the humanity or the deity of Christ:

> Many deceivers, who do not acknowledge Jesus Christ as coming in the flesh, have gone out into the world. Any such person is the deceiver and the antichrist. *2 John v 7*

But there is so much more that comes from the truth of Jesus' humanity. We have a Lord who reigns in heaven who understands our condition; he can sympathise with our struggles and suffering and physical frailty. As the writer to the Hebrews puts it:

> For this reason he had to be made like them, fully human in every way, in order that he might become a merciful and faithful high priest in service to God, and that he might make atonement for the sins of the people. Because he himself suffered when he was tempted, he is able to help those who are being tempted. *Hebrews 2 v 17-18*

But often overlooked is what Jesus' humanity reveals about *our* humanity.

So let's draw everything together by exploring precisely how Jesus perfected humanity, taking the three categories we have already thought about. Because Jesus was perfectly human, **he shows us what we were created to be** in the life he lived on earth. More than that, **he shows us the life we will be restored to in** the new creation. And finally **he shows us *shalom***: the possibility of everyone and everything living in blissful harmony and perfect relationships.

1. Enjoying *shalom* with Father and Spirit

Here's a puzzle. What was it about his death on the cross that was so hellish for Jesus as he prepared himself in Gethsemane? After all, many faithful disciples down the centuries faced their martyrdom with composure and confidence. Take the first martyr, Stephen. As the crowd, overseen by the future apostle Paul, hurled those fatal stones, Stephen had a vision of heaven, knelt to pray and fell asleep! Consider the 21 Coptic Christians beheaded by ISIS in February 2015. As Beshir Kemel, brother of two of the martyrs, said: "They died courageously with the name of Jesus on their lips," and in full confidence of his imminent presence. *What made Jesus so different?*

The physical and emotional torment of crucifixion was clearly horrendous. But others have endured similar, if not worse, fates. *The answer lies in Jesus's spiritual life.* He was anticipating the horror of horrors: separation from his Father for those hellish hours on the cross. We can never plumb the depths of that agony because we can never grasp the beauty of their intimacy. Yet this intimacy is what he would forfeit at the cross... for us.

While it is a mistake to try to split Jesus into divine and human sides, we can certainly see aspects of his spiritual life that reflect humanity as it can and should be. He showed what *shalom* with the Father and Spirit looks like. He reveals a spiritual life that we can and should aspire to, as the proper expression of being human.

a. Jesus was constantly dependent

Like the deep-sea diver dependent on her oxygen supply, Jesus constantly spent time with his Father. For him it was a life-and-death matter; right from the outset, Jesus is seen getting up before dawn to pray, retreating to isolated spots, sometimes for whole nights. The more hectic his work, the more he spent time in prayer.

But it wasn't just private spirituality. As he had done since childhood, Jesus would observe the Jewish festivals, like Passover or Tabernacles. He would regularly join synagogue services on the Sabbath. He was clearly concerned for the temple to be honoured and used rightly. Less publicly, he might spend time with his disciples in prayer or singing (Matthew 26 v 30).

He longed for the joy of his relationship with God to be shared by those he came to serve. That was the whole point! How can we live and thrive without God? Individually and corporately, time with God and dependence on God are both essential to being human.

b. Jesus was constantly obedient

Even though his own authority was obvious, Jesus never undermined the authority of the Jewish Scriptures. That meant keeping the law's commands perfectly. But he also fulfilled the law's purpose and spirit.

Still, Jesus was sometimes accused of undermining the law—as with the Sabbath laws—as if he was some kind of progressive liberal. Ironically, he insisted that the law was actually *more* demanding, not less, than his critics believed it to be—so "do not murder" is fundamentally a challenge to curb anger. If anything, Jesus was as critical of the Pharisees' dilution of the law's demands as their hypocrisy about keeping them. That explains his repeated contrast between their teaching, and his own in the Sermon on the Mount (Matthew 5 – 7).

Ultimately, in the law, God had revealed his "Maker's instructions" for human flourishing. Watering them down or altering their purpose inevitably brings harm, not freedom. For Jesus, obedience was never a resented burden but a daily joy; it was true *shalom* with his Father and the Holy Spirit, not an irksome trial.

It has been said that loyalty only begins at the point of disagreement. So it is with obedience. That makes Jesus' Gethsemane prayer all the more powerful. Jesus was terrified. He longed for an alternative, for "this cup [to] be taken from [him]" (Matthew 26 v 39). And yet, he could still say: "Not as I will, but as you will". He had to go to the cross—it was essential to his mission and to fulfilling the Scriptures.

So here is the paradox: it is at the cross that we see Jesus' true humanity fulfilled—a life lived in perfect obedience and *shalom* with the Father and Spirit culminated in the obedience of his death.

It was not the end, of course.

The Father restored him to the highest place. But the cross is where he truly earned Paul's title for him as the last or ultimate Adam. Jesus was the first human being truly to live at peace with God. He lived and died to win our peace.

2. Enjoying *shalom* within himself

I remember hearing how a professional scriptwriter

first got intrigued by Jesus. He'd spent years on the hunt for writers who could manage to create a convincing good person. It's much harder than you might think. Too often, they seem rather pathetic and wet, or too good to be true, or self-righteously masking some secret flaw. At best, they're just bland and dull. Baddies with sinister flaws or schemes are far more compelling, which is why actors relish getting their teeth into those roles.

Unaware of this interest, a friend suggested he read one of the Gospels. The impact was immediate. The Jesus he encountered was utterly believable, not *despite* his goodness but *because* of it. In fact, the more he read, the more he sensed that he could never have been manufactured—it would have been impossible to get it right. Fact is far stranger than fiction, but in this case it is also more credible.

Nicky Gumbel captures Jesus's perfect goodness well:

Here was a man who exemplified supreme unselfishness but never self-pity; humility but not weakness; joy but never at another's expense; kindness but not indulgence. He was a man in whom even his enemies could find no fault and where friends who knew him well said he was without sin. Surely no one could suggest that a man with a character like that was evil or unbalanced?

Questions of Life

Nothing proves this better than the kinds of friends he attracted. You might think it was religious types who flocked to him. After all, their lives were "better", weren't they? Their failings would seem less exposed by comparison with Jesus' goodness. Yet from the start, it was religious people who plotted his downfall. It was society's dropouts and moral failures who couldn't get enough of him. People today usually assume that Christianity is only for religious types—this just shows how far short of Jesus' example many of his followers fall.

I have a hunch that this was one of the secrets to Jesus' magnetism. He was completely at ease with himself. This God-man with flesh and skin was comfortable in his own skin. He had no intimidating hang-ups or instabilities. He lived in perfect holiness without ever seeming to be "holier than thou".

a. Jesus was perfectly integrated

Jesus could be unpredictable—it's one thing that makes him so compelling. People would watch in amazement as he unexpectedly dodged threats while pulling off miraculous feats and acts of supreme kindness.

But for all his unpredictability, Jesus was always consistent. Everything about Jesus operated in harmony, with body, mind, and soul working in perfect co-ordination. Everything he did served his mission in obedience to the Father. He always knew exactly where people were coming from and so knew what they needed (even if it wasn't what they wanted to hear). His character might be complex and his teaching profound, but no one discovered a single gap between his words and actions. Not once.

This is the result of Jesus' mastery of the virtue that modern Christians seem to value the least: *self-control.*

b. Jesus was perfectly self-controlled

When I'm tired, I lose perspective and become doom-laden. When I stub my toe, I shout at the closest victim to hand. When I'm drowning in deadlines, I'll dash work off as quickly and carelessly as possible. Self-control is something almost everyone struggles with. But we *never* see that in Jesus. He never snapped, he never retaliated, he never lost his nerve—even when at the end of his tether, physically, emotionally or spiritually. This is how we are meant to be.

Yet again, he proves this at the cross. Despite knowing *exactly* what would happen there, "Jesus resolutely set out for Jerusalem" (Luke 9 v 51). He controlled his fears to do what he wanted, needed, had to do. And even as he hung on the cross, he had the presence of mind to use his last remaining ounce of energy to ensure his mother would be cared for by John. The *shalom* he experienced within himself enabled him to live out *shalom* with the Father and Spirit, and also with others.

3. Enjoying *shalom* with others

All sorts loved being in Jesus' company, and he clearly enjoyed being with them. How else can we explain the charge of being "a glutton and drunkard, a friend of tax collectors and sinners" (Matthew 1 v 19). Despite carefully guarding his alone times, he was never isolated or lonely—except at the very end. Those closest to him let him down. But he never let anyone down. He was a reliable and trusty friend.

We can see this in many ways—but perhaps the simplest is to see how he lived out the two key ideals that the ancient prophets longed to see in God's people: justice and love.

a. Jesus and justice

Victims of injustice invariably live at the bottom of life's ladder. The more powerful people are, the more they can get away with.

Jesus well understood the power dynamics of his society—he knew who was in control, but was never afraid to speak to power. He was appalled by the hypocrisy of the Pharisees, who were blind guides and whitewashed tombs, "who shut the door of the kingdom of heaven in people's faces" (Matthew 23 v 13-36). They were powerful, but defenceless against his charges.

Luke in particular tells how Jesus gave special attention to those on the margins: the sick and disabled, the poor or enslaved, the women and children. He would hardly have done this unless he was aware of their low status and vulnerability.

But Jesus was not an inverted snob. He was open to all who would come to him, including the rich and powerful, like Nicodemus or Joseph of Arimathea. It's simply that he was no respecter of worldly or religious status—he treated *everyone* equally and impartially. But in God's restored community, that is precisely what we would expect to find.

b. Jesus and love

Of course, where such a community is not found, what does he do? He subverts it all by abandoning all his privileges and rights. He becomes the menial slave who strips to his underwear, gets on his hands and knees, and washes his disciples' feet, verrucas and all. It's undignified—and really quite embarrassing for everyone concerned. But this is what the disciples needed at that moment. So that is what Jesus did for them. Because he loved them. Regardless of the cost of that love.

Which means we must return one final time to that supreme act of love: the cross. At Golgotha we see his greatest act of service.

> For even the Son of Man did not come to be
> served, but to serve, and to give his life as a ran-
> som for many. *Mark 10 v 45*

This is humanity at its most noble and generous.

> Greater love has no one than this: to lay down
> one's life for one's friends. *John 15 v 13*

This is the kind of love human beings were made to give. It is the kind of love Christians are saved to give. The result of such love is true *shalom*—peace with God; peace with ourselves; peace with the world and creation.

When Queen Victoria was on the throne of England, she heard that the wife of a labourer on one of her estates had just lost her baby. Having experienced deep sorrow herself, she called on the bereaved woman one day and spent some time with her.

After she left, the neighbours asked what the queen had said. "Nothing; she simply put her hands on mine, and we silently wept together." This was not Victoria the queen. This was Victoria the grieving mother. Victoria the human being.

In Jesus we meet a King of infinitely greater authority and power. But also in Jesus, we meet someone who is one of us. He shows us what we can be. And he saves us to become what we *can* be: to become the people in God's image that we were always created to be.

So what does make us human?

As should be obvious by now, sound-bite answers to this question are risky and usually unhelpful. What's more, any answer that is confined to our physical and material reality will always be fatally flawed. We can't grapple with human nature without grappling with God.

In essence, we are human because the Creator God made us human. And so his revealed plans are *essential* for answering the question. We have much in common with the rest of the created world, especially with mammals and apes in particular; but we are so, so much more. We are made in God's image.

This means that in order to express our true humanity, we need to invest in all three of these life dimensions:

■ **The divine dimension.** We were created to live for the one who made us. As Augustine said centuries ago, *"You have made us for yourself and our hearts are restless until they find their rest in you."* Not only do we find our ultimate fulfilment in relationship with God, but we find the only true stability in a turbulent world. As the psalm writer said, *"my God is my rock, in whom I take refuge."* (Psalm 18 v 2)

■ **The personal dimension.** We were created in a complex but integrated harmony of body, mind and soul. In their different ways, each contributes to our humanity. None is superior to another, but each is necessary. Giving us bodies was no reluctant afterthought on God's part. We thrive best when each part of us is fit (physically, intellectually and morally).

■ **The social dimension.** We were created to live in various concentric circles of relationship with others. We grow best when we relate best to others who are equally made in God's image. As theologian Andrew Wilson puts it, *"You cannot honour the President while burning an effigy of him. You cannot honour God while despising an image of him. Love your neighbour."*

It is obvious that each of us fails in each dimension. We are limited, flawed and failing. There is so much about each of us that undermines our created humanity. But this is the wonder of the gospel. In Christ, we find not just the perfect example of humanity—in all three dimensions—but the greatest hope for humanity.

As a result of his doing for us what we could never do for ourselves, we are brought back to our Creator and gradually restored to what we were made for. The day will come when we are transformed in the twinkling of an eye, to be perfect, integrated, holy.

Dag Hammarskjold was the second Secretary-General of the United Nations, but was also a follower of Christ. He once said,

"I became a Christian in order to become man."

He clearly understood that, far from limiting or restricting us, trusting in Christ is the greatest decision we can ever make. For how else will we ever be restored to what God made us to be?

thegoodbook
COMPANY
Opening up the Bible

At The Good Book Company, we are dedicated to helping Christians and local churches grow. We believe that God's growth process always starts with hearing clearly what he has said to us through his timeless word—the Bible.

Ever since we opened our doors in 1991, we have been striving to produce resources that honour God in the way the Bible is used. We have grown to become an international provider of user-friendly resources to the Christian community, with believers of all backgrounds and denominations using our Bible studies, books, evangelistic resources, DVD-based courses and training events.

We want to equip ordinary Christians to live for Christ day by day, and churches to grow in their knowledge of God, their love for one another, and the effectiveness of their outreach.

Call us for a discussion of your needs or visit one of our local websites for more information on the resources and services we provide.

UK & Europe: www.thegoodbook.co.uk
North America: www.thegoodbook.com
Australia: www.thegoodbook.com.au
New Zealand: www.thegoodbook.co.nz

UK & Europe: 0333 123 0880
North America: 866 244 2165
Australia: (02) 6100 4211
New Zealand (+64) 3 343 2463